Bagan

Bagan

Words and photographs by Barry Broman

Book Promotion & Service Co., Ltd.

ISBN 1-84464-001-9

Copyright © Book Promotion and Service Co., Ltd. 2004

Published in Thailand by
Book Promotion and Service Co., Ltd.
2220/31 Ramkhamhaeng 36/1
Huamark, Bangkok 10240
Thailand
Tel: +66 2 7320243-5
Fax: +66 2 3752669
E-mail: booknet@book.co.th
Distribution:
UK & Ireland:	Paths International Ltd.
	P O BOX 4083
	Reading, Berkshire
	RG8 8ZN
	U. K
	E-mail: pathsmail@aol.com
Rest of the world:	Booknet Co., Ltd.
	1173, 1175, 1177, 1179 Srinakharin Road
	Suan Luang, Bangkok 10250
	Thailand
	Tel: +66 2 3223678
	Fax: +66 2 7211639
	E-mail: booknet@book.co.th

Design: Pimmas Suksri

Printed and bound in Thailand by
Amarin Printing & Publishing Public Company Limited

All rights reserved. No part of this publication may be reproduced, stored in a retrieval system, or transmitted in any form or by any means, electronic, mechanical, photocopying, recording or otherwise, without the prior permission of the publisher.

Bagan ...

China has its Great Wall. Cambodia has Angkor Wat. Indonesia has Borobudur. Myanmar has Bagan, a city of temples on the banks of the Ayeyawady River.

Myanmar (formerly Burma) is often considered the hidden pearl of Southeast Asia yet it is far less known and less travelled than any of its neighbours. It has been a crossroads for civilisations as seen in the diversity of its people and their cultures. Strategically located between India and China and bordering Bangladesh, Laos and Thailand, Myanmar has had a turbulent history of invasion and internal struggle. Throughout much of that history, the city of Bagan (formerly Pagan) has been fought over, conquered and suffered earthquakes, but has somehow survived.

Sitting serenely on the banks of the Ayeyawady River (formerly Irrawaddy), Bagan was the first Burman kingdom. It arose in the tenth century, supplanting the Pyu kingdom, but did not become a power in the region until the reign of Anawrahta (reigned 1044-77) who extended the power of Bagan over much of what is today Myanmar.

Anawrahta directed a massive construction effort that can still be seen. At its zenith in the 13th century, there may have been more than 6,000 Buddhist temples and stupas at Bagan and many more wooden structures that are long gone. Today some 2,000 stone and brick structures remain, many of them recently repaired. A few of the greatest retain a major role in the daily life of Myanmar's predominately Theravada Buddhist religion. Bagan thus remains a centre of Buddhist worship with major festivals drawing large crowds of devout adherents from throughout the country and abroad.

Despite the ravages of war and time and the destructive influence of the river that has eroded as much as one third of Bagan's area, life continues in and around the temples and stupas. Stupas are solid structures usually sited on a square or pentagonal base. Temples are built with internal chambers for the placement of Buddha images. They offer mute testimony to the long and rich culture of the people of Myanmar who created the magnificence of Bagan.

The Pyu: an enigmatic people

Little is known about the Pyu; who they were, where they came from, or what happened to them. It is known that the Pyu were a Buddhist civilisation that rose along the Ayeyawady River early in the first millennium of the Christian era and that they controlled the upper Ayeyawady valley in competition with the Arakanese and Mon. Gradually Burmans moved into the area from southern China and eventually came to dominate the region.

The ancient walls of Bagan, which still exist in part, date from the middle of the ninth century. About this time the Pyu kingdom fell to the kingdom of Nanchao based in southern China. Out of this turmoil rose the Burman state of Bagan which carried on the strong Buddhist traditions of Pyu and Mon culture. Inscriptions at Bagan were largely written in the Mon language until the twelfth century.

One of the oldest pagodas in Bagan, Bu Paya, dates from the Pyu period and today sits on the banks of the river although originally it was further inland. It was destroyed in the 1975 earthquake but has since been reconstructed. It is a landmark for river travellers.

Bagan grew in size and power under the Pyu, Mon and Burmans but did not achieve greatness until the reign of King Anawrahta in the eleventh century. It was his zeal for conquest and construction that led to the golden age of Bagan and his legacy is seen today in some of Bagan's largest and most revered temples.

The prototype for Burmese stupas for the next thousand years was the Shwesandaw Pagoda, credited to Anawrahta and built around 1070. This is the first pyramid-shaped stupa in Myanmar and was built to house a hair of the Buddha

King Anawrahta is credited with fostering the spread of Theravada Buddhism throughout his kingdom and especially at his capital, Bagan. Credit for the king's conversion has been given to a young monk named Shin Arahan from Thaton in lower Myanmar on the Gulf of Martaban.

The story goes that when Shin Arahan was a young man he travelled to Bagan where he lived as a hermit on the Bagan plain. At that time religion in Bagan was a mix of spirit worship, Mahayana Buddhism, and other beliefs from India. King Anawrahta heard of this young monk and sent for him. Brought into the king's presence, Shin Arahan boldly sat upon the king's throne, an act that should have brought his immediate execution. Instead, the king was impressed by the audacious monk and soon became a devoted adherent of Theravada Buddhism and a patron of Shin Arahan.

In his zeal for the new religion, King Anawrahta asked King Manuha of the Mon kingdom of Thaton for copies of the *tipitaka* Buddhist scriptures. King Manuha refused. This refusal had a profound impact on the history of Myanmar and on Manuha's own fate. Anawrahta attacked and conquered Thaton and brought Manuha to Bagan as a prisoner. Imprisoned at Myinkaba, a mile south of the walls of Bagan, Manuha erected elegant examples of Mon-style temples.

One of these is the Manuha Temple, built in 1070. It houses four large images of the Buddha, including a large reclining Buddha on his deathbed. It is said that the cramped spaces inside the Manuha Temple were intended by King Manuha to reflect his own confinement in Bagan.

Kyansittha's gift to posterity

Although Anawrahta is remembered as the unifier of Myanmar, conqueror of the Mon, builder of temples, and champion of Theravada Buddhism, it is Kyansittha (reigned 1084-1112) who is acknowledged as Bagan's greatest king. A great warrior, Kyansittha married a Mon princess, Khin U, and continued the massive construction works of his father. Using the talents and skills of 30,000 captive Mon who were brought to Bagan, Kyansittha's Bagan was known as *the city of four million stupas*.

Of all the magnificent pagodas and temples of Bagan, a few are particularly celebrated. Chief among these is the Ananda Temple, widely considered the finest surviving example of Mon architecture in Bagan and the greatest gift that Kyansittha left to posterity. Dating from the late eleventh century, this may be considered Bagan's first great temple. In recent years it has been renovated and repaired, as has much of Bagan. Today the temple's gilded *sikhara* or crown, topped by a round stupa, rises to a height of 168 feet.

Inside the temple are four vestibules, each housing a 31-foot-high standing Buddha image carved in teak and covered with gold. The Ananda Temple is a centre for Buddhist pilgrims as well as tourists and every January at the time of the full moon, a festival is held that attracts faithful Buddhists from all over Myanmar. Located just within the walls of Old Bagan, the temple is perhaps Bagan's most ethereal and beautiful. Legend has it that Kyansittha was so impressed by the singular beauty of the building that he personally executed the architect so that it could not be replicated or surpassed.

Not far from the Ananda Temple is the 200 foot high Thatbyinnyu Temple, Bagan's tallest. This twelfth century temple is known as the "temple of omniscience." It was never finished. The Thatbyinnyu Temple is considered the archetypal Burman style of architecture and is one of the finest contributions to the beauty of Bagan from King Thatbyinnyu (reigned 1112-67), who succeeded Kyansittha. In a departure from the Mon style of architecture, the Thatbyinnyu features a Bamar innovation, a small hollow cubed second storey atop a solid base. The temple is graced with a large Buddha figure facing eastward. There are also a variety of seated gilded Buddha figures along its galleries.

Narathu murders King Alaungsitthu, his father

The history of Myanmar's kings, Buddhist though they may have considered themselves, is one of murder within the royal family, a tradition that continued right up to the end of the independence of Burma in 1885, when Mandalay fell to British soldiers. So it was with the death of Alaungsitthu at the age of 81. He was murdered by a son, Narathu (reigned 1167-1170) who smothered the king as he lay on his deathbed. Narathu promptly claimed the throne and had himself crowned while his elder brother was away.

Perhaps as atonement for killing his father, Narathu began construction of Bagan's largest temple, the Dhammayangyi. The massive structure was built in the same Greek-cross pattern that characterised the Ananda Temple. Legend records that Narathu personally oversaw its construction and if he could pass a needle between the bricks he would have the mason responsible executed. The temple rises in six terraces, a mountain of brick that shines red in the sundown of Bagan. It is still in excellent condition today, perhaps a testimony of King Narathu's extreme measures to assure high-quality construction.

Narathu himself had a short reign and like his father, was murdered. The king had taken his late father's wives as his own after the death of King Alaungsitthu in accordance with the custom of the day. One of these women, a daughter of the Indian Prince of Pateikkaya, incurred the wrath of Narathu and he had her executed. This in turn angered her father who sent eight assassins disguised as Brahmins to Bagan. When they were received by Narathu, they drew swords and killed the king. Then they killed each other. Thus another reign in Bagan was truncated in bloodshed.

Kublai Khan seals the fate of Bagan

By the middle of the thirteenth century the Mongol hordes of Kublai Khan had swept across China and into Southeast Asia. In 1273 ambassadors from Kublai Khan arrived at Bagan demanding that King Narathihapate (reigned 1254-87) send a royal prince or senior minister to Peking as a symbol of Bagan's subordinate status to China. The king was not disposed to send a hostage to China and he was offended by the Chinese envoys' refusal to take off their shoes as demanded by custom. Narathihapate ordered the ambassadors killed, thereby setting the scene for the end of Bagan as the centre of Myanmar's political and cultural life.

Kublai Khan took revenge for the deaths of his ambassadors and made war on Bagan in a series of campaigns that ultimately caused King Narathihapate to destroy hundreds of stupas to build defences in an effort to stop the Mongols. Nevertheless, Bagan fell and although the Mongols did not destroy or loot the city, they put an end to Bagan's greatness. The future kings of Myanmar ruled from elsewhere.

The Venetian traveller Marco Polo visited Bagan at about this time, giving us the first Western description of the city. He said that "... the City of Mien [Myanmar] was a very noble city and in it were 'towers of stone' covered with gold and silver and bells at the top inasmuch that whenever the wind blows among these bells they tinkle."

The Bagan that Marco Polo visited must have been magnificent, a vibrant, cosmopolitan city bustling with trade and the rich arts and crafts that befit a growing empire. Temple walls were often decorated with murals depicting the lives of the Buddha or other religious scenes. Some of these paintings can be seen today, usually in an advanced state of destruction. To protect them, many of the smaller temples are locked but guides can access these little treasures, if asked.

The fall of Bagan to the Mongols brought an end to the city's role as the political centre of an empire, but it continued to be the cultural heart of the country and in some ways that tradition endures today. Major temples have been restored over the centuries despite serious depredations. The Ananda Temple continues to be an important pilgrimage site as are the Shwezigon and Manuha Temples. There is a rich religious life in and around Bagan, notably at Sale, located twenty five miles to the south, with its beautiful wooden monasteries and colonial architecture.

Bagan is the centre of the lacquerware industry

The ancient art of lacquerware continues to be concentrated at Bagan where thousands of artisans are today taking this art form in new directions. Classic black or cinnabar red lacquered offering vessels, *hsun ok*, are produced in much the same way they have been for centuries. A bamboo woven frame is covered with raw lacquer paste. After drying in special subterranean rooms the piece is sanded and more layers of lacquer are applied.

Sometimes lacquer is applied to a wooden base, or in the case of the highest quality drinking cups, a framework of woven horsehair. In addition to a broad array of colours now available in the lacquerware shops, artists incise the hard shiny lacquer with ornate designs that are either geometric or depict a religious scene. Full sets of dinnerware are produced, as are screens, trays, tables and a wide array of containers including those traditionally used for making food offerings to monks.

The lacquerware industry revival in Bagan has rejuvenated the environs of the ancient city. A new town south of the archaeological park is bustling with lacquerware workshops where visitors can watch the complete process of lacquer being made. The same shops offer decorative and functional wares, usually sold by young sales ladies wearing thanaka, the white cosmetic that Myanmar ladies of all ages adore.

On the banks of the Ayeyawady River just east of Bagan lies the town of Nyaung-U which is the centre of commerce for the area with its port and nearby airport. The British crossed the river near here in 1944 in their successful effort to retake the country from the Japanese. Nyaung-U features a large and lively daily market where the matrons do their daily shopping. Here one can find jaggery, a delightful product of the sugar palm which dot the Bagan plain. Here too there is a growing section devoted to the sale of antiques, and crafts, especially lacquerware. Puppets are also in evidence, as are bronze tattoo implements, or a hundred other items for the visitor who must haggle hard for a reasonable price.

The heat and especially the low humidity of the "Dry Zone" of middle Myanmar has been kind to Bagan by preserving its hundreds of stone and brick structures. This aridity also protects, to some extent, the delicate painted murals inside the temples. Even a few wooden statues from the days of Bagan's greatness have survived, thanks again to the dry heat. Much of the damage inflicted by the massive 1975 earthquake has been repaired and in recent years, there has been a major effort on the part of the government to restore many of the ruins.

For the traveller, there has been extensive construction of new and better hotels. Cruise ships now ply the meandering channel of the Ayeyawady. Jet aircraft bring visitors in an hour from Yangon or only twenty minutes from the new international airport at Mandalay. For better or worse, Bagan has been discovered by the world and its great charm and beauty acclaimed. Despite the construction, renovation and easy access to the outside world, Bagan still travels at the pace of its pony carts and the city of temples on the Ayeyawady continues to evoke awe and reverence.

plate 1 :

A nat at the Shwezigon Temple.

plate 2 :

A guardian lion or chinthe at the Shwezigon.

plate 3 :

Novice monks at the Shwezigon Pagoda.

plate 4 :

The Shwezigon was begun by King Anawratha and completed by Kyansittha in 1087. Tradition says that the holy tooth, collarbone and other relics of the Buddha are enshrined in the Pagoda.

plate 5 :

The Shwezigon Stupa. It is not clear if Kyansittha was the son of King Anawratha.

plate 6 :

Carving at the Shwezigon Pagoda.

plate 7 :

Gold abounds at the Shwezigon. Shwe means "gold" in Myanmar.

plate 8 :

The Shwezigon from the Ayeyawady River. Its zedi (tower) represents Mount Meru, the centre of the universe. Perhaps as much as one third of Bagan has been reclaimed by the river over the centuries.

plate 9 :

The Ananda Temple in early Bagan style was built by King Kyansittha in 1105.

plate 10 :

The Ananda rises gracefully from this antique land. The temple is said to represent the endless wisdom of the Buddha.

plate 11 :

Buying Buddha images and religious paraphernalia at the Ananda Temple fair, a major annual event.

plate 12 :

Lacquerware at Bagan.

plate 13 :

One of four standing Buddhas at the Ananda Temple. They are 30 feet high. Those facing north and south are original. The others were destroyed by fire and subsequently replaced.

plate 14 :

The Ananda Temple. Two footprints of the Buddha are found on pedestals in the west porch.

plate 15 :

The golden spire of the Ananda Temple.

plate 16 :

Details of a doorway at the Ananda Temple.

plate 17 :

Roof detail of building at the Ananda Temple.

plate 18 :

Stucco figures enliven a Bagan pagoda.

plate 19 :

The massive Dhammayangyi built in the Mon style by King Narathu in 1160. It has the finest brickwork of Bagan.

plate 20 :

Twin Buddha images at the Dhammayangyi Temple.

plate 21 :

The Gawdawpalin Temple was built during the reign of King Narapatisithu (1174-1211).

plate 22 :

Traditional transport for a novice monk.

plate 23 :

Ladies too smoke cheroots and collect the ash in a coconut shell bowl.

plate 24 :

Temples on the Bagan plain, the dry zone of Myanmar. The arid climate has helped preserve the temples and their decoration.

B a g a n

plate 25 :

Stupas in every direction.

plate 26 :

A Buddha image in Bagan.

plate 27 :

A restored pagoda. Many have been restored following damage by earthquakes and the passing of time.

plate 28 :

Temples rise from the lush foliage of the welcome summer rain.

plate 29 :

Making lacquerware at Bagan in the same style as past centuries.

plate 30 :

Lacquerware is the main cottage industry for Bagan families.

plate 31 :

Making lacquer trays, a process that takes weeks to complete.

plate 32 :

Antique lacquerware for sale. These are hsun-ok vessels made to carry offerings to temples.

plate 33 :

The Thatbyinnyu Temple, also called The Omniscient, is a fusion of Mon and Bamar styles. It is widely considered the most splendid temple of Bagan.

plate 34 :

A gilded Buddha image at the Thatbyinnyu Temple.

plate 35 :

The tower of the Thatbyinnyu Temple. It is the highest in Bagan rising to 61 meters (200 feet).

plate 36 :

Stupa, right, and ruins of a monastery. Despite their antiquity, many monasteries flourish in Bagan.

plate 37 :

Stupas in the early morning.

plate 38 :

Stupas at Bagan.

plate 39 :

Mural depicting a boating scene.

plate 40 :

Rural life continues in much the same way as when the temples were constructed.

plate 41 :

Bullock carts and foot power ensure the harvest reaches homes and markets.

plate 42 :

The Ayeyawady is both a transport artery and an alfresco bathroom.

plate 43 :

Young lady wearing the popular thanaka cosmetic. Thanaka protects and nourishes the skin. It is made from the ground bark of a small tree.

plate 44 :

The Bu Paya stupa, shaped like a gourd, is one of the oldest shrines in Bagan. It may date from the 3rd century AD.

plate 45 :

The Bu Paya on the bank of the Ayeyawady. It was destroyed in the 1975 earthquake and later rebuilt. It is a landmark for riverine traffic.

plate 46 :

In all directions, temples and pagodas...

Bagan

plate 47 :

Dawn at Bagan on the river.

plate 48 :

Stupas, known in Myanmar as "zedi".

plate 49 :

The Shwesandaw Stupa, one of the few tourists are allowed to climb. It once housed images of Mahapeinne or Ganesha, the Hindu god of wisdom.

plate 50 :

The old ways of travel are still the best.

plate 51 :

Less venerable pagodas crumble into the earth from whence they came.

plate 52 :

The immense Buddha at the Manuha Temple.

plate 53 :

Buddha image in the Manuha Temple.

plate 54 :

The Ayeyawady River is a lifeline for Bagan's residents.

plate 55 :

The only way to cross the river is by ferry, known as Z-craft.

plate 56 :

Stucco on a zedi.

plate 57 :

An ogre frozen in stucco.

plate 58 :

Stucco preserved by the dry climate of the plains.

plate 59 :

Shops at the Ananda Temple fair.

plate 60 :

Burmese puppets at the Nyaung U market near Bagan.

plate 61 :

The Mahabodhi Temple took its style from the Vajrasana Temple in Bodh Gaya, India.

plate 62 :

Detail of the Mahabodhi.

plate 63 :

Stupas, stupas and more stupas

plate 64 :

Buddha image at Bagan.

plate 65 :

The Thein of U Pali is an ordination hall. Interior decorations are probably from the 18th century.

plate 66 :

A family carved in wood at a monastery in Salay near Bagan.

plate 67 :

Bullock carts are often the only transport. The palms are a source of alcoholic toddy and jaggery (raw sugar), Myanmar's favourite confection.

plate 68 :

A delicate carved figure in a niche of a Bagan pagoda.

plate 69 :

Bagan-style painting created by one of the many young artists who work in Bagan.

plate 70 :

Temples and stupas dot the Bagan plains.

plate 71 :

The passage of time and several earthquakes have damaged many pagodas. Here they are being restored.

plate 72 :

A monastery, one of many, punctuate the Bagan plain.

plate 73 :

More stupas and monuments than one can count.

Bagan

plate 74 :

More monuments...

plate 76 :

Ancient pagodas and stupas coexist with 21st century farms.

plate 36 :

Bagan at dawn.